QUICK MONEY MANAGEMENT TIPS

How to Save Money, Pay off Debt, and Have Financial Freedom

D.C. Phil

ISBN-13: 979-8-6658-4588-3

Printed in the United States of America

DISCLAIMER

This book contains opinions and information based on actions and behaviors that worked for and helped the author. The opinions and information presented in this book are the author's own and do not reflect the opinions of any organizations that the author may be affiliated with. The information provided is accurate and true to the best of the author's knowledge, but there may be omissions, errors, or mistakes. There are no guarantees or promises being made regarding the accuracy of this information.

The opinions and information presented in this book are for entertainment and/or general informational purposes only and are not intended to provide any kind of advice, including specific advice or recommendations for any individual or on any specific security, stock, bond, or investment product. If readers rely on any opinions or information in this book, it is at their own risk.

Nothing in this book constitutes investment advice, performance data, or any recommendation that any security, stock, bond, portfolio of securities, investment product, transaction or investment strategy is suitable for any specific person. The author is not a financial advisor and cannot assess anything about your personal circumstances, your finances, or your goals and objectives, or your individual situation, all of which are unique to you. Any opinions or information contained in this book are just that – an opinion or information. The opinions and information found

For my Parents.

CONTENTS

INTRODUCTION

When I started out on my own, I was at the classification for poverty-level and stayed there for many years due to the debts caused by the 2008 market crisis. I had to get down to the basics and figure out the best way to improve and secure my financial situation. Thanks to analysis, trial and error, and help and guidance from my parents, I succeeded in this endeavor and am financially solid now. So, I decided to share the information regarding what worked and helped my situation.

In this book, I want to give you a basic introduction to money management, which I feel is a topic that we are not really taught about in schools or, in some cases, even at homes. Sure, you might have had a consumer education class required in your high school, but not all states have that requirement, and most people nowadays grow up with no financial guidance whatsoever.

There are many long-lasting financial traps, such as debts you cannot easily repay, that you can fall into just by going about your daily life and making financial transactions without realizing the full scope of what you may have entered into. On the other hand, if you have a developed awareness of money management and the topics related to it, you can begin moving in the right direction and make your financial life much more bearable. In fact, when you are finally in full control of your financial situation, you will develop a sense of inner peace and confidence created by having a full awareness of your situation and the ability to successfully respond to and adapt to any challenges and changes to it.

So, let's begin.

PART ONE

THE BUDGET

To better understand your financial situation, you can first make a thorough budget of all your sources of income, expenses, and debts. The primary idea behind this is to make visible and identify every way that money is coming in or going out. On this budget you can even include a goal you want to work towards. For example, if you are saving money for a purchase larger than you would make on a daily basis, such as a car, you can use the budget to determine how much you would have to allocate to that plan to be able to achieve it.

If you have numerous open accounts, credit cards, mortgages, and other loans, then you would want to have a way of keeping track of everything – the amounts owed, the minimum payments, the due dates of each minimum payment, and so forth. At this point, you can even use apps on your phone to do this for you. Although it can be very helpful to use software that lets you complete and update a spreadsheet, you do not actually need any apps, software, or even a computer for this. It will be enough to have a pencil, eraser, and a notebook or even just a sheet of paper large enough to include all the information you need. However, if you have a phone that can get one of the free spreadsheet apps available now, then you have a method of conveniently updating your information as you go.

If you have lots of accounts spread out at different financial institutions, you may find it timesaving and more convenient to find a way to get them all into the same financial institution of your choice. This is not a strategy for everyone, because, at certain times, some financial institutions will offer more competitive rates, products, and investment strategies than the ones offered by others. However, there are people who could potentially benefit from having to check only one place for the status of all their savings accounts, checking accounts, money market accounts, CDs, mortgages, other loans, IRAs, Roth IRAs, credit cards, and other financial products that people usually get from various, unconnected financial institutions.

Finding a way to get them all or, at least most of them, transferred into one financial institution instead of numerous ones will also cut down on the number of user logins and passwords you would have to keep track of. If you are using online banking, make sure to also use two-factor authorization or some other way of making sure that no one can access your account(s) with just your login and password alone.

Once you have this all sorted out and organized, what you really want to look for first is to see how well your income covers your expenses. If your expenses exceed your income, then you could look for more ways to expand or increase your income, but it is usually much faster and more attainable to decrease your expenses wherever and whenever you can, eliminating, at least for the time, any expenses that are outright unnecessary or contradictory to your goals. There are many ways to reduce expenses and some will be mentioned later on in their own chapter.

If, on the other hand, your income surpasses your expenses, then you can still look towards reducing or eliminating superfluous expenses. This will have the effect of increasing how much money you can keep for your own benefit. One example of such a benefit would be that you would have extra money to spend on whatever goal you are focusing on. Another example would be that you could put the extra money to immediate use by paying extra on any debt you might currently have, in order to pay if off at a faster rate.

You might have heard that you should save anywhere from 10% to 50% of your income as savings. Being able to save at least 50% is considered an ideal goal. However, in practical terms and depending on what the situation is with your expenses, you would want to save as much as possible and definitely want to move as far away as possible from a situation where you have 0% going towards your savings, while expenses use up 100% of your income.

An idea behind this is to first set aside money for yourself, before paying any out for any other purpose. It might help to see this process as making a payment to yourself first. This does not, however, mean to take a portion for yourself in order to spend it on some unnecessary thing, such as extra clothing you did not need or a meal more lavish than you needed to eat. Rather, it means that, when you get your check, you automatically reserve a portion of it for your savings. If you do it the other way – by waiting after you have paid everyone else and only then seeing if there is anything left for your savings – then the chances are that you will not find much or anything at all left at the end.

If this continues, then long periods of time can go by before you get to the point of having savings set aside for yourself. So, what you would want to do instead is to automatically take a percentage of that money you earned and save it. After that is done, the remainder can be used to pay bills and you can live off the rest. Pick a percentage to set aside and stick to it. Some money is better than none.

In my situation, I kept it simple and as long as I saved more than I had to spend, that was enough. I did not make it complicated with in-depth formulas or precise percentages applied to all categories, and this simple method worked just fine for me. Until you get to the point that you are, by habit, saving more than you spend, you can basically monitor all your transactions on a case-by-case basis. Given that sometimes you may find yourself in the situation where you have no choice but to spend more than you earn, keep a look out for those transactions where you can, after all, save more than you spend, or save all and not spend at all. The idea behind this is to win as many of the small victories as possible, in case you find yourself in the situation where you cannot yet win the bigger battles. As long as you can consistently come out ahead by keeping more money than you have to part with, you have a way to improve your situation with a beneficial, long-term habit.

If you are very meticulous and thorough, to the point that you want to and are able to successfully keep track of every cent that you earn or spend, then you can more easily scrutinize your expenses to see what you really do or do not need to spend money on. Try doing this for a few weeks and you will get a clearer idea of where your money is going and what you can do to try to change that. If you are just starting this today and wish you could see what you have already spent money on in the past, then you can actually check your credit card statements and bank account statements to see what the transactions were for your credit cards and debit cards. At the same time, you could look through your receipts to see how you spent your cash.

Once you look over all your transactions in detail like this, you will be able to identify items, or even entire categories of purchases, that you could do without. Even if it turns out that you still need those items or categories, you can still see if you are spending more than you need to for them. There may be better deals available by now that you can pick instead of what you currently spend the money on. A simple example is to see if another store, maybe even one nearer to you, sells the exact same type of item, but at a lower price, making it more affordable and increasing its value in that way.

It would be good if you can keep your budget sheet frequently updated. Ideally, you would update it as soon as you have a transaction, no matter how small. However, if that is not possible, then try to do so once a week, once a month, or at least a few times per year. It is a good practice to maintain. The important thing is to be able to be as aware as possible of what your situation is, so that you are able to get to that point where you have more income than expenses. Seeing your own progress can energize and motivate you to continue working on your goal and see further improvements.

DEBTS

Once you are at that point where you have more income than expenses, then if you have any debts, you can use the extra amount to pay off the debts more quickly. There are two classic and well-known strategies for doing this. You may have even learned about one or both of them from a family member, as I did. In case you have not heard of them already and are unfamiliar with them, then this chapter will tell you about them.

The reason these strategies are classic and well-known is because they are effective and successful. In one method, you pay off the smallest debts first. Once the smallest debt is paid, you take the amount of money that you used to pay for that debt, and you add it to the amount you are paying for the new smallest debt. Consider the following example.

If the smallest debt you have requires $10 of minimum payment each month, and the second smallest requires $40 each month, then in the final month of the smallest debt, you would pay $10 for it and $40 for the second smallest one. Once the smallest debt is paid, you take the $10 and add it to the $40 to start paying $50 for the second smallest debt, which has now become your new smallest debt. It is critical that you do not spend that $10 unnecessarily for other reasons, but that you assign it to your debt payments until all your debts are cleared. Also, on the $10 debt, since that is the smallest one and you would be focusing on it, you would also want to try to pay more than just the minimum whenever and as often as you could. Instead of spending extra money on purchases that you do not need at the moment, any extra money you have available would be used to add to the $10 in order to pay off that debt as fast as possible.

Keep repeating the practice after you finish each debt and in the end you will be hitting that last debt hard, until you finally settle all accounts. This method is good for motivation, because you pay off debts faster and faster until you are done, and you feel the satisfaction that this causes. I personally picked this route because it felt as if I was speeding through the process and finishing off the debts much faster.

The other method is where you pay off the debts in order of interest rates, because you are going after the debts in the order of which one costs you the most money each month. This method is also supposed to free up a significant amount of money over time, because the most expensive monthly payments are being cleared. Whether you choose this method or the previous one, you pay only the minimum payment per month for all the other debts until it is their turn to become the focus of your payment strategy.

What you can also do is use any extra money you get to pay down the debts. Ignore the desire for a quick impulse purchase and just use any windfalls or extra money you worked hard for, such as holiday pay, towards the debt payment plan you picked. This will work to your advantage, assuming you do not already need to use the money for some other necessary expense. Remember, also, that this extends beyond just the debts from financial institutions and can apply to situations where you owe another person money. There may not be a formal contract with them, but it is a debt if you owe them money.

Once you have paid off a few debts, especially if they had a combined minimum payment of a few hundred dollars, then it will feel as if you suddenly have a lot more money. The best way to use that money is to continue with the strategy until your debts are paid off. It would not be helpful to splurge on some sort of reward at this point.

An even worse case would be if you get in the habit of spending money on things you would not have before because you could not have, because the newly-freed money being used to buy such things was previously being allocated only to the debts that you paid off. In other words, you would not want to make a new habit of splurging just because a little more money is now available. Rather, you would have to keep yourself disciplined and follow through with your plan. You already made this much progress and would not want to risk falling back into a bad state.

In the worst case, if something happens that you did not expect or have plans for and you suddenly need the extra money, it would be unavailable and you would no longer have access to it if you already spent it all buying unnecessary things. Specifically, if something happens and the situation becomes so severe that you are worrying about paying your water bill, or electric bill, rent or mortgage, or even a medical bill, then you would see the benefit of having that extra money available. That would not be the case, however, if you had already spent it acquiring a bunch of things you did not need urgently, but that you bought on the spur of the moment just for fun.

It is far better to make sure all accounts are settled first. Incidentally, having debts cleared from your list of worries can lead to significantly better sleep, which is a satisfaction and a benefit worth having, in and of itself.

Whichever of these two strategies you pick, time ends up being on your side because you make more progress towards clearing your debts as time goes on.

Now if you do not have large debts, but just smaller, revolving monthly debts from your credit cards, then it would be good to pay those off in full by the due date, to avoid fees, such as late fees, and interest payments on the balances. This is to help prevent them from turning into major debts, as high interest rates on balances can accelerate that process significantly. The two strategies mentioned in this chapter can also be used to pay off credit card debts, regardless of their size.

When you are clear of debts, try to go on without getting into any debts ever again. It seems as if everyone is very desensitized to debt and takes it for granted that they will have huge debts, that their parents and most of the people they know have or will have enormous debts. Yet, if you made it to this point, you will know that it is not true that you absolutely have to have debts in life.

Debts will keep you down and can drastically alter your future in a way that you would not choose if you knew that you can live and be happy without ever having debts. If you do get into debt at this point, after finally clearing off your debts, it would either be the type of small, monthly credit card revolving debt that you then pay off in full before the due date, or it would be something you are fully prepared and are able to pay off responsibly, that you know you have control over and that serves your purpose, rather than something that keeps you down for decades or the entirety of your life.

If you are still paying student loans, getting a mortgage on top of that can be harmful. It depends on a case-by-case basis, but it is generally not helpful to take on more loans when you already have debts. Getting into debt for a brand new, luxurious car is also not worthwhile. Vehicles lose their value relatively quickly, but the debt you have entered into in order to acquire the vehicle will stay with you until you pay if off. By now, people are also starting to consider whether or not getting into tremendous debt for college expenses is the best choice, if they do not have a guaranteed job waiting for them afterwards which will pay them what they need in order to enable them to quickly and fully settle the debt.

EMERGENCY FUND

A s mentioned earlier, if something unexpected happens that requires you to be able to pay a lot of money, then you will find it helpful to allocate some money to an emergency fund. The number of months of backup, emergency money you want to keep on hand is at least a few months to half a year. Ideally, it is at least one or two years. However, it really depends on your situation and you would want to save as much as you think you would need for yourself and for those you care for and who depend on you.

When you consider how high hospital and other medical bills are nowadays, that can give you an idea of what amount of money you would need if you were not able to work and had little to no income for months. You would factor the expenses for all necessary purchases and services into this – meaning, rent, utility bills, groceries, phone bills, insurance, and other purchases and services you need to spend money on to maintain every month. If you are able to set aside a year or two's emergency funds for yourself, then that would be one less thing for you to think about in the event you actually need to put those funds to use.

The amount of money needed to set aside an emergency fund may seem enormous at first. However, if you keep at it and keep setting aside money for it whenever you can, then it will gradually add up and you can meet the requirement that you established.

Paying off your debts will aid in this endeavor, as will saving money consistently.

You would also try to reduce your monthly expenses as much as possible. Then, after a year or two of consistently setting aside money for this purpose, your emergency fund should have a substantial amount of money, especially compared to if you did not save any money at all for this category.

PART TWO

EXPENSES

This chapter on expenses will contains various ideas of what categories of expenditures a person can look at to start finding ways to cut down on costs, whether the costs are daily, weekly, biweekly, monthly, or even yearly. Some information regarding expenses is mentioned in other sections, for which reason only information that has not yet been primarily focused on or presented in detail will be found in this section.

Bargaining:

One way to reduce your costs would be by improving your ability to bargain. This does not mean to cause difficulties with store managers and store employees about small, everyday purchases. However, if you are buying a car, yacht, house, or some other very expensive item, then it can help to try to negotiate with the seller for better terms or for a more affordable price.

In fact, even computers and other modern technology can fall into the category of very expensive items now and it does not hurt to try to negotiate reasonably with the one selling the item. There are many ways to develop your negotiation skills. There is one thing to be aware of and to stay clear of: specifically, overly enthusiastic and argumentative negotiation can easily cross the line of what ethical and moral if it becomes clearly disadvantageous or harmful to the seller. You would not be trying to make your situation worse, but you would also not be trying to cause harm, financial or otherwise to the seller. That is to be avoided, as the idea is for the agreement to at least be mutually beneficial.

Bottled Water:

Elsewhere in this book, coffee is used as an example of where you can save time and money by making certain changes. Similarly, bottled water is another category. Instead of buying bottles of water, you can buy a reusable, durable, high-quality bottle and refill it. It would be a one-time purchase meant to last through many, many uses and you would only have to clean and maintain it, rather than throw it away. You would also save time and money by not having to frequently go to the store to buy multiple, heavy cases of water bottles either.

This is one idea that would be able to save money for people who have reliable and consistent access to clean, filtered water, but end up buying bottled water anyway. If the water you have at home is clean, filtered, and safe to drink, then you would only have to refill your reusable bottle with that, which would, in that way, save you a significant amount of money each year in terms of that reoccurring purchase. Moreover, the less plastic you purchase and dispose of, the better it is for the environment. You would be helping to save the planet.

Buying Brand Names:

We usually buy products with certain brand names because of an expectation of superior quality. As it turns out, many generic products have identical or very similar ingredients or compositions to the brand name product. The main difference is that the generic name product is less expensive.

For consumable items, you can check and compare the list of ingredients and the food labels to see if there is any real, substantial difference between the generic product and the brand name product. Sometimes you can even buy a greater overall quantity of the product if you buy the generic version, if, for instance, the brand name version is two times the price. As an example, you were planning to spend $5 on a product. The brand name version is $5.00, but the generic version is $2.50. At this point, you can buy the generic product and save $2.50 for some other purpose or use. You also have the option of buying two copies of the generic product instead. In this way, you would be getting the product you need, but at a better and more affordable price.

Buying In Bulk:

If there is something that you routinely buy and need, you can consider buying it in bulk if it is less expensive to do so. This can also save time because it would reduce the frequency with which you may need to repurchase the item.

If you live by yourself or are only buying those supplies for yourself, then buying them in bulk with also cause you to have a bigger supply of the product for longer. Also, since it is something you normally buy, you can benefit by finding coupons or other deals for it.

Clothes:

Simplifying your choice of clothing can save you money. This does not mean you would have to go to an extreme end of wearing the same clothes every day, but it would mean that you would not be at the other extreme end of buying a new outfit to wear one time and never again.

If you can pull yourself away from the thought that you have to constantly show off how expensive your style is, then you would also feel more able to move away from the thought that you have to keep coming up with a style that is constantly better and more expensive.

Fashion goes out of season, but simple, practical clothing can last and serve you well for a long time and through many occasions.

Coffee And Other Daily Purchases:

There is another category of reoccurring charges that can be seen in the case of habitual, daily purchases. For example, if you spend $3 a day on coffee, every day of the year, then you would be spending 365 x $3 = $1095 on coffee alone every year. It will be more if you spend more than $5 or if you buy coffee multiple times a day. If you also buy other consumable items every day as well, then this figure goes up quite a bit more.

Given the nature of the item, you may not be willing to eliminate it from your daily consumption. However, there are still ways to reduce the costs associated with, in this case, drinking coffee every day. For example, you can brew your own. Furthermore, depending on how you make it, the process may take about the same amount of time or may even be faster than if you had to wait in the line at the coffee shop every day, in which case you would benefit by saving both time and money. Little things can and do add up. Win all the small victories you can in this regard, and you will be better prepared for the bigger financial battles.

Cooling:

In terms of cooling, if you do not have restrictions in place against doing so, then you could consider planting trees or having them planted to shade your house is a natural way and to reduce how much heat affects it. You would have to take other things into consideration, such as if severe storms and winds would make the trees a danger to your house, or if insects and animals can now use the trees to get to your roof and then into your house in some way. Provided that these issues are nonexistent or are manageable, then the solution of planting trees of having them planted could save you money on a long-term basis.

Furthermore, when planned correctly, the addition of well-maintained trees to a property generally makes it look better and can have a favorable effect on its value. If you live in a region where the trees lose their leaves during the fall, allowing more sunlight to reach your house, then that could help with warming it up during the colder seasons, which would allow you to save money on heating.

Getting darker curtains for use during the summer and keeping the curtains closed during the brighter parts of the day can reduce the amount of heat entering your home through direct sunlight.

If you like being out of the house, then you have other ways to stay cool during summer, including swimming at the pool, or spending time in libraries and other public places with indoor air conditioning.

Other ways to save on cooling would be to not set the temperature too low during summer.

Costly Products And Services:

If you barely have enough money to get by and are not close to being financially stable, then you would not want to buy expensive technology and other gadgets. You can also find an alternative to expensive weekly manicures and pedicures, designer clothes, shoes, purses, and make up from department stores. It is better to be rich than to temporarily create the image of being rich.

If, however, you do still have to buy such things, wait until near the end of a month or whenever the sales representatives' deadlines are for meeting their quotas, because they are, in general, more likely to give you a better deal or a greater discount near the end of their required period, if they still have not met their quotas. This can also be helpful also with more expensive purchases, such as cars. However, this way of going out things may not always succeed, though it can still be an option to try. If you are merely trying to take advantage of the salesperson and the business to their detriment, however, then that would no longer be fair, acceptable, or reasonable.

Coupons:

Coupons are useful for reducing the amount of money you would spend. Where you can, it would be good to use coupons. At the same, it is good to consider whether or not a purchase is being made simply because a coupon exists for it and it seems to be a deal too good to pass up. In other words, would you normally buy that item, or are you buying it because you found a coupon for it?

If it is an item that is normally purchased, then the coupon saves you money. If it is something that you had no intention whatsoever of buying, but are only doing so because there is suddenly a coupon or a deal for it, then you would be spending more money than you had planned to.

In such a case, if you did not get that coupon, you would have kept that money and would have been able to put it to other uses. This becomes more clear in cases where people buy things that they never use, just because it seemed to be a good deal at the time and they felt as if they would miss out if they did not buy it.

Credit Cards:

When it comes to your credit cards, it would be better to only make purchases with them that you know you already have or will have the money to pay for before the due date. It would be good to pay the balances of any and all credit cards in full by or before their due dates, to avoid fees, such as late fees, and to also avoid interest payments on the balances. It is also better to get or switch to credit cards that do not have unnecessary fees, such as yearly fees. Try to get lower interest rates as well, if possible. Also, keep in mind that the more preferable credit cards also tend to have rewards.

Some cards have better rewards than others and those would be the ones to go for. For example, getting cash back or getting a statement credit can be helpful and useful towards your revolving, monthly credit card balances. The reward of an unnecessary item will not help as much, unless you allowed to and can legitimately sell if for more money than you would have gotten through a cash back or statement credit option.

Moreover, what you want to avoid is making purchases with your cards just for the rewards, because it is often less expensive to just directly buy the item than to accumulate the large amount of points needed to get the item as a reward.

Once you have successfully built up enough reward points, you would want to consider using them while you still can and before they expire. To better be aware of when the points expire, it would be good to keep track of the expiration dates of different points, because some cards have systems where only certain points expire at certain times. Ideally, you will have picked a card where the reward points do not expire at all.

Education:

Some work-study programs at colleges and universities allow you to reduce the cost of your tuition. Also, if you know you can transfer your credits from a local community college to the university of your choice, then you would be able to benefit from the less expensive, but equally valid courses at the local community college. In all cases, it would be good to check that the institutions you are planning to attend are properly accredited.

Electricity:

Energy-efficient lighting can reduce your electric bill. Even just switching out the most used lights in your home with energy-saving lightbulbs, such as CFLs, LEDs, and halogen incandescent, and other energy-saving options can reduce overall yearly expenditures on electricity. You will have to pay some money out the first time that you buy them, but they will then save you money over the years, when compared to what you would have been spending with the traditional type of lightbulbs.

Another practical way to save money with lighting is to simply turn off the lights when you no longer need them, such as when you are not in the room at all and there is not anyone or anything in the room that needs the lights to be on.

You could also connect your devices to a power strip and then switch off the power strip when you do not need to use the devices. This is because, as long as they are plugged in, your devices will continue to use electricity, even if no one is using them. The more electricity the devices need, the more your overall yearly expense increases. Having less electricity running through your devices may also have the potential to extend their lives.

Employee Discounts:

See if you can get a discount just by being an employee. This is useful if you or a family member will be allowed to purchase a product or service at a lower price. Many industries, including universities, hotels, airlines, gas companies, internet providers, and car rentals, to name a few, have such arrangements.

Food:

Someone who is trying hard to save money would benefit from not eating out at expensive restaurants frequently. Even fast food, when bought daily and multiple times a day, has the potential to offset any savings you are accumulating. Instead, it is better to make your own meals.

Also, if the food item is something you eat all the time, consider buying it in bulk if it is possible and if that saves you money to do so. In this case, the use of coupons would help, because it is for a purchase that you would normally make anyway.

If you have the time, learn the recipes of your favorite meals, so that you can make them at home at a lower cost than eating out.

Grocery Shopping:

Do not go shopping at the grocery store when you are hungry. Rather, eat ahead of time so that, when you go grocery shopping and are passing by food, you are more likely to avoid making an impulse purchase. This is because, when you are hungry, you may be more likely to buy food that attracts your attention, even if you did not originally plan to buy that food ahead of time. This is more likely to happen simply because the hunger is influencing your decision.

It becomes a more focused issue when you are in the checkout line for a long time and have to wait next to or nearby many types of snacks. You can reduce the likelihood of making an impulse purchase at this point by eating ahead of time or, in fact, by preparing a food purchase list ahead of time and sticking to it no matter what. This way you would buy only what you intended to buy, rather than what you felt like buying at the moment, due to hunger.

Heating:

As for heating, you could keep the temperature lower than normal or just plain not set the temperature too high during winter, and then wear socks, head coverings, and even an extra layer of clothes if needed. This would also depend on whether or not you could do so without putting yourself in a precarious situation in terms of health.

When the heating system malfunctioned and I did not have heat in the middle of winter during heavy snowstorms, I ended up wearing all my winter clothes and multiple layers of clothes and socks inside the house, while sleeping under all the bedsheets and blankets that I had, until the heating system could finally be repaired. This happened two winters in a row because of the heating system failing. However, lowering the temperature severely is not a recommended situation to be in. I had no choice in the matter and the above situation of lowering the temperature is based on the concept of lowering it only to a degree that is still reasonable and that is still safe.

Other ways to save on heating would be that you could insulate your attic to help lower heating costs. You can even insulate your windows. Adding a door draft stopper can help block cold air from entering your home during the winter. At the same time, the door draft stopper can help prevent cold air from exiting your house in the summer.

Hired Services:

If you have the time and ability to mow your lawn, wash your car, clear your leaves, clean your home, clean your gutters, shovel snow or use a snowblower, watch your children, walk your dogs, then consider not hiring expensive companies to do this for you. However, if you do need these services, then consider family and friends whom you can trust and rely on who might be willing to do them at a lower price or maybe even for free.

Hobbies:

If they are not essential and you can do without them, you can consider having cheap hobbies instead of very expensive ones. You would not have to keep to this decision forever, but it can help you in the beginning if you are trying hard to save money.

Housing:

Housing costs can be very high, perhaps the highest or one of the highest of your expenses. If you are young and your parents are ok with it, consider moving back in with your parents. If you already live in the same city, then you find that you may not have to move very far. If you are the parents and are ok with your child moving back in, then there would be the additional benefit of having another person bringing income into the household, while the overall burden of the bills could be reduced by having another person contribute to their payment.

This idea works even if you are related more distantly or not even related at all. By combining households, people can reduce the overall number of bills – one set of utility bills, not two; one homeowner's insurance bill, not two; and so forth. This would increase the value of everyone's income, because no one person would any longer have to pay the entire burden of the costs of living by themselves, and everyone would be able to keep more of their own money for themselves and for their own personal use. There are other benefits to combining households, including the opportunity for increased and improved social relationships, and less overall use of resources, along with the corresponding effects that has on the environment.

This idea is not to be abused, with one person or party exploiting the situation and being the only one to benefit, despite having joined someone else's household. In the case of children rejoining their parents' household – there is a cost for the accompanying increase in utilities and groceries. Everyone would have to do the right thing and contribute. It would have to be that each person's presence and participation in the household is a benefit, not just to themselves, but to the other members of the household as well. No one should be exploiting the generosity of the ones who let them join their household.

You would just have to ignore the stigma the western world has regarding this, where everyone must go their own way, whether they can afford it or not. That may have worked in the mid 1900's until the end of that century, but times and conditions have changed greatly. Families and cultures in other parts of the world have not required that the family break up as soon as possible, with each person moving out to do their own thing, whether they can financially afford to do so or not.

Instead, families have stayed connected or even together, which succeeded in strengthening the families. After all, when you are keeping more money in your own family and not spending it unnecessarily on multiple sets of the same type of bill, then you are strengthening your family's overall financial position. If, in addition to doing this, you continue the various practices of financial discipline and teach them to your children, then you are setting your descendants up for success.

However, if you are only doing this temporarily and are set on having your own place, then you need to be actively saving money the whole time you are relying on and contributing to the household that is allowing you to live with them. You would want to be financially strong and to be able to take care of yourself, without having to rely on others.

If you do not have the option of moving in with your family, consider your friends. If that is not an option, you can look for roommates, or you can rent out a small room. If it is possible, you can even get a roommate for that small room, further splitting costs. Without a roommate, you would go for the cheapest, smallest room that you find convenient and reasonable, because having a smaller space can make you less likely to want to buy a whole bunch of furnishings and other items that would only end up taking up more of your space, which would make it more uncomfortable for you to stay there. Being in a small room may be uncomfortable, though that may also motivate you more to improve your situation so that you could move out. As long as you are consistently and reliably improving your savings and financial situation, no matter how difficult it gets, then there would still be that hope available that eventually things can improve.

On the other hand, if you have a big house with lots of extra rooms, you could look into renting them out. You could even look into renting out storage space in your garage or extra rooms. There may be insurance and safety considerations, along with lease and other contract considerations to look into, but you could find out about those and see if you are still interested in the idea.

Internet:

Most people seem to no longer have the option to choose from different internet providers. So, they are not able to pick the most competitive plan. However, you can still check with your current provider once in a while to see if there is some new deal that you can switch to or take part in.

If you do not want to spend money on paying for the internet at all, you may be able to use the internet at your local library once you are a member.

A middle point between these two options would be to see what your options are for a mobile hotspot. While the data limits may be more restrictive depending on what plan you choose with your mobile hotspot, this option is, at the time of this writing, far less expensive in the long run than the traditional internet option. You would have to monitor your use and data limits, but you would also be able to take your connection to the internet with you as you move about.

Late Fees:

Even if you only pay late fees once in a while, they are still fees that you would not have to pay when you are better organized and better aware of your financial obligations. So, avoid paying late fees that you are charged due to merely forgetting to keep track of due dates and making the required payments on time.

Laundry:

This idea would be one to consider in a case where every last penny is critical. Specifically, the idea to consider would be whether or not doing your laundry where you have to pay 25 cents for it is better than doing it in your house, where it might cost you more in terms of your electric bill and in terms of your water bill.

Even if you do use your own washer, then maybe it would be better and would save you more money to hang the clothes to dry, rather than using the dryer. If you do not use your own dryer, but hang the clothes to dry, then you might also consider that such an action is said to have a degree of beneficial impact on the environment. Finally, perhaps you feel enterprising and, where it is allowed and reasonable, would want to charge other people, who do not have their own, a fair price to use your washer and dryer when you are not using it yourself.

Membership Fees:

This topic is discussed in the section on Subscriptions and Membership Fees.

Miscellaneous:

If you start thinking in terms of your hours worked vs. the cost of what you are buying, it can change your perspective. Suppose you make $10 an hour and are considering buying a $200 item. That is the same as working 20 hours to buy that item. That calculation is based on your gross earnings, before federal taxes and, if applicable, state taxes, which means that it would actually take you more than 20 hours to buy that item when the calculation is based on your net earnings. Even if the item is actually $10, when you think about how hard you worked for that $10, it might change your perspective on whether or not the item is something you want to buy, especially if you do not even need it. What you do every day will either bring you closer to or take you farther from your goals.

Try to have days where you do not spend any money at all. It can be one day a week, or more if you can get by without a problem. The savings you accumulate from not purchasing anything on such days can add up nicely after a while. This does not include the bills and other financial obligations that you must pay, but only concerns those extra items that you do not necessarily need to buy. If you become adept at this, maybe try to go longer than a day and see how you get by.

Since you know you will have to set aside a certain amount of money for rent and bills, then you could consider keeping that money aside where it is readily accessible but still earning interest. Then you could pay on time, but closer to the due date. On the other hand, if you are more likely to spend that money on things that it was not meant for, then you may benefit from paying your rent and bills as soon as you can.

Phones:

If your phone is functioning perfectly well and there is no practical need for a newer one, then you can consider keeping your current phone, instead of buying an expensive new one every year. On top of that, if you do not want to use the major phone network providers, there are less expensive alternatives available. For example, you can even buy a prepaid phone that will require you to only purchase more minutes as needed.

A prepaid phone is also good for those who do not want to be in a contract that lasts for years. Moreover, with no contract, you can switch to a different provider if you do not like the one you are currently with. Mixing these options – using a smartphone, but with an alternative service provider that does not charge a high monthly fee – can save you some money every month.

A final word on this topic is that, if you do not need to do so for work purposes, it would be better not to unnecessarily have two phones for yourself, leading to two sets of bills from the same category but for only one person.

Purchasing Multiple Copies Of Forgotten Items:

Plan ahead of time so that you do not end up buying something you already have at home, but that you ended up buying another copy of, only because you did not take it with you when you went out. As an example, see if you will need your sunglasses ahead of time and then take the pair you have at home with you instead of buying a new pair while you are outside.

This also applies to other things, such as your lunch. Make sure you do not forget your lunch, thus finding yourself required to buy a more expensive, and possibly less fulfilling one, outside.

Another example of this is the purchasing of umbrellas. Know ahead of time by finding out ahead of time what the forecast for rain is so that you will know if you will need your umbrella later in the day. Do not forget it, only to then end up buying another one later that day while you are outside because you got caught in a downpour.

Even if you make such purchases infrequently, they are still purchases that you would not have to make when you are better prepared and remember your items.

Second-Hand And Shared Items:

If you need to purchase an item and do not mind that somebody else already owned it, you can look for deals first, rather than buying it brand new at the full price that brand new items are first sold at. By now, there are several websites and apps you can use for this purpose.

You can find many items from all kinds of categories on Amazon. Other than that, there are options spanning from eBay and Craigslist to Letgo and OfferUp. You can even look into local thrift shops. Some of the services available now have built in ways that allow you to negotiate and bargain for better deals.

If it is something that you only need once a week, like a lawnmower, then maybe you and a neighbor can come to an arrangement where you borrow or rent their machine for a day. If neither of you have a lawnmower, maybe you can split the cost to purchase one together, with whoever needing it keeping and using it for the moment. It would be more cost-effective than both of you having your own lawnmower that is used only once a week. Arrangements could be made for how and when it will be maintained and for when and how it will have its oil refilled, along with the other concerns of that nature.

This idea can be extended beyond just lawnmowers, to snowblowers, vacuum cleaners, garden tools, ladders, and other items that sit idle for most of the week or longer. If everyone cooperates in this arrangement and there is no abuse of it, then the shared item ends up being more affordable, providing more value to more people.

Purchasing refurbished items and products can also allow you to have a high-quality item at a much lower price. You would have to check relevant descriptions and conditions or used or refurbished items.

Subscriptions And Membership Fees:

Are there subscriptions that you no longer need? Maybe there are things you signed up for that were useful once, but no longer serve the same purpose, so that you can do without them. Subscriptions of this sort include a monthly membership to something that you have not used for months and do not need, but that maybe you did not realize was still actively charging your card every month.

Even if it is an amount that seems low, such as $10, think about it this way: at the end of a year, that will be $10 charged 12 times, resulting in $120 that you could have saved. Here is another important aspect to consider about this: if you have several of these $120 reoccurring charges per year (let us say four of these types of subscriptions), then that is 4 x $120 = $480 per year that you can save. On the face of it, you would not be willing to spend $480 in such a way if it was obvious; but if dismiss the charges, thinking of them as being only $10 a month here and there and go on to think that $10 is not so much, then you will be more likely to accept these charges in your finances. As a result, their costs will continue to add up in this way by the end of the year, without you necessarily being aware of their full effect on your finances. So, look at any extra costs and see if you can save the money for them instead, because all these small expenses add up fast and that is money that you can reclaim for yourself.

I had this experience with a gym membership. At first it was great to be able to go to the gym for only $10 a month. At the time, comparable gyms were about $30-$50 per month and were farther away. So, this gym was not only more affordable, but it did not take as long to get there, even though it still was a little distant from where I was living.

Everything was fine at first and I could go several times a week if I wanted to without any problem. Eventually, once enough people found out about the gym's relatively low membership fee, it got to the point where the gym's parking lot was so packed full of cars that people risked parking tickets and towing, because they were parking on the grass and in the main road, despite the signs posted there saying that such parking was not allowed. Inside the parking lot, people risked accidents over the scramble for parking spots.

When it got to the point that I could no longer even park when I went to the gym, but had to turn back because there were no reasonable alternative options available at all, I went ahead and cancelled that membership. It was worth the benefits to my fitness and overall well-being to spend the $10 a month, but it was not worth paying any amount for something that was not even possible to use. As a result, I had $120 extra per year available to me.

Before leaving this subject of cancelling memberships, let us consider one possible fee that you may be unexpectedly required to pay: the cancellation fee. Take a look at the fine print of any memberships or subscriptions to see if they charge you an extra month or two after you cancel. That happened with the gym membership, where they charged the following month's fee, even though the following month was weeks away.

Be aware of such a possibility, especially if you were expecting the extra money to be freed up and available, only for it to turn out that you actually have to wait a little longer, because there were terms to that effect written in the fine print.

Targeted Advertisements And Promotion Emails:

If you find yourself making a lot of purchases online or in person after seeing advertisements online, then you could consider using a private browser or clearing your browser's history regularly, because you may be the recipient of targeted advertisements that are the result of having your browsing history tracked. These may then go on to suggest certain products and services to you as a result.

Targeted, personal advertisements can be useful if you happen to be made aware of something that you wanted to buy but did not know existed. However, if they are, instead, a frequent source of prompting for an expenditure unnecessary to you, then you can make a habit of clearing your browsing history to avoid targeted advertisements. Similarly, if you get emails that target you specifically based on what you buy, which then increase the frequency with which you make unnecessary purchases, then it would be better not to be subscribed to such emails.

However, these targeted advertisements and emails, if they give you discounted rates, are still a good choice if you normally purchase that item or service anyway and would thereby be saving money. They would not be good in the case that you unnecessarily make purchases that you had no intention of making and that you only made because you happened to see the advertisement or email.

In the same line of thought, sometimes websites upcharge you if you are browsing while logged in. If you were not logged in and the website did not identify you, then you may have been shown a lower price.

Taxes:

There are many credits and other ways to reduce taxes owed that many people do not know about. For example, people may be aware that getting into their employer's 401(k) plan will directly reduce their taxable income. Another benefit of this would be if the employer contributes a matching amount. However, the same people may not know that they may now also qualify for a small tax credit just for making retirement contributions.

It is helpful to know how and when you can legitimately reduce your tax burden. The richest people do not necessarily have the knowledge themselves, but they are known to hire very knowledgeable accountants and attorneys who specialize in this field and are able to find ways to significantly reduce their taxes owed. It could be a helpful category worth looking into.

Utilities In General:

Utilities are a reoccurring monthly expense that you would want to minimize as much as legitimately possible. This includes everything from checking out competitor providers' rates, if that is an option, to selling your house in order to move into a smaller house, because smaller houses generally require less heating and cooling, and because they also usually require less electricity.

Water Bill:

If you turn off the tap and do not keep the water running when you are brushing your teeth, shaving, or using the sink in some other way, then you can lower your water bill and save some money. If the water does not need to be running, then the tap can be turned off until you need to use the water.

This concept applies to utilities and other such costs in general. In the case of water, you could turn off the tap to save money when you do not need the water. In the case of electricity, you could turn off the lights to save money when you do not need the lights to be on. Practices that save on utilities also generally benefit the environment.

Vehicles:

Your vehicle may be a source of continuous expenses for you. What you can do to save some money is to learn some basic, very basic, mechanical knowledge, such as how to replenish the various fluids your vehicle needs and how to check on the tires and tire pressure yourself. You could even learn how to change the oil yourself, without having to go to a mechanic for that. Knowing how to and being able to safely take care of things like that can save you time and money.

On the other end, if the car has gotten too old, chances are that its various properties and systems are wearing down and the vehicle needs frequent repairs. I kept my vehicle in great condition, but it was already old and got older. Eventually I found myself having to pay for hundreds of dollars of repairs every few months.

No matter how well you take care of your vehicle, the longer you use it and the older it gets, the more likely you will find yourself having to pay for costly repairs to it for systems that newer vehicles would not need to have repaired as frequently.

If insurance is costly, you can shop around for better rates from other companies. If you are a student or the parent of a student whose insurance you pay for, you can find out what the GPA requirements are from your insurance company for a good student discount, if they have one.

If you use your vehicle to drive short distances, consider walking or using a bicycle instead. Many people prefer to drive half a mile or just down the block, even if the weather is clear and the area is safe to walk or bike through. Numerous short trips of this nature add to the gas and the gradual wear-and-tear costs of maintaining your vehicle. Also, though it is not always possible, if you can live near where you work, saving time and money from not having to make long commutes is a great benefit.

As far as long commutes go, if your hourly wage is $8, once other pertinent factors are considered, it may not be worth the gas costs of driving to a distant location to work. Maybe there are similar jobs closer to where you live. Maybe you can find a way into a different field of work that pays better and is also closer to where you live.

On the other hand, if you can take the train or bus safely, then you could do other things during your commute, such as reading books you have been interested in. You would have spent that time travelling to your work anyway, but now you could spend that same time doing something else that you enjoy.

Other things to consider are that vehicles are depreciating assets that lose value as soon as you drive off the dealer's lot. With that in mind, there is really no good reason to buy a fancy, brand new car if you are trying to save money. As long as the car you are buying meets safety and other standards and can get you to where you need to go reliably without frequent repairs, then you would be able to get by with a used vehicle.

It would help you to save money if you also got one that was fuel-efficient but also resistant to heavy damage in the event of an accident. A vehicle that is more resistant to damage, has the potential to reduce the likelihood of your getting seriously hurt and needing expensive medical procedures for yourself and extensive repairs for your vehicle.

You can also save money if you decide to buy the vehicle outright, with cash, rather than getting into debt with a loan. If a loan is necessary, it can be helpful to check your options ahead of time and be preapproved, instead of relying only on the dealer's financing options. If you were able to get all your financial products transferred to the same bank, as described in the chapter on debts, then you would also have an existing relationship with the bank that may be to your benefit when it comes to financing a vehicle loan.

Finally, negotiating with the dealer during the price discussions can help your cause as well. After all, if you can lower the purchase price, then you would be reducing the overall amount you would need to be financed for.

CONCLUSION

Some Brief Comments on the Perception of Money

You can succeed if you stay dedicated to your financial goal. Even if you stray from your path every now and then, as long as you get back on your path as soon as possible and persevere to the end, you will be able to achieve your goal.

You would not want to end up financially unstable late in your life, as a result of impulsive decisions made earlier in your life. Among other things, you may simply not have the physical capability or opportunity to work as hard in your later days, as opposed to your earlier days, to undo the mistakes of costly, impulsive decisions. You would want to retire in peace, and without having to worry about money at that time.

You will have to resist the idea that "you only live once" or that you are missing out if you do not spend all your money in a lavish way by making significant purchases, because the chances are good that, after you return to your budget sheet and update it, you will regret the decision to break with your plan and, in worse cases, you may become demoralized to the point of giving up on your goal.

You would also have to move away from the beliefs and habits you developed that caused you to see it as normal to overspend. Maybe there was a time that you only bought something expensive once a month but then started buying it more frequently because you could, until, through this pattern, you finally got to the point where you started buying it every day and you became accustomed to such expenditures. This will be a pattern that you would have to work on undoing.

You have to replace unhelpful patterns that you have become desensitized to regarding money, with ones that will help you achieve a better financial situation. Even if it is hard at first, if you do it long enough and it becomes your primary mindset, then not only will you become accustomed to living more frugally, but may even begin to enjoy it and to feel satisfaction from it and the accomplishment of having control over your finances.

At the minimum, your shelter, food, physical comfort and security, ability to obtain and pay for medical help, as well as your manner of recreation will, as long as it is physical or relies on technology, depend to some degree, usually a significant degree, on your ability to securely and consistently be able to fund it and to be financially stable. One other point to note is that, even if you do not plan to use the money for yourself, you can still help others with it by feeding them, providing for them, or even creating a business that hires and pays them, which in turn allows them to feed and provide for themselves and their loved ones.

There is a very old concept that money is the root of all evil. In reality, money is just a means to an end – it is the medium by which we enable or disenable ourselves to operate within our society, by its rules and processes. If you see a person suddenly "go bad" after getting money or becoming a lottery winner who goes bankrupt, then the real problem was not in their obtaining the money, but in their not soundly managing their financial situation. Any problems they had were already part of their character and in them, undealt with, but amplified and unrestricted by the freedom they received after gaining the money. The character flaws did not suddenly develop from out of nowhere. Rather, they were already present there all along, just subdued by the daily hardships of life.

In your case, your goal would be to stabilize your situation so that you can live comfortably and continue your lifestyle the way you want to live it, while being able to handle any challenges that come your way, without having to really worry about them. If you become very successful at this, you may even find it possible to retire earlier than the current, expected retirement age and still be able to live the way you would prefer. Changing and getting control of your habits now is what will eventually be the deciding factor as to whether or not you become rich or poor. The earlier you make the necessary changes, the better.

Comparing Lifestyles:

More specifically, it is not helpful to any degree to compare your own lifestyle to those of celebrities, people you know or follow on Facebook and Instagram, or any of the people you see in Reality TV shows. In the case of Reality TV, the people you see on those shows are usually not starting from the same position you are in. For the most part, they have either pulled themselves out of that situation and are in a position of success, or they were never in that situation in the first place. Even if you happen to find one where the person is in a similar position, your situation is your own and comparing it and your challenges to someone else's will not, except for in the case of drawing motivation from them, benefit you in general.

As for celebrities, they, for the most part, have the financial resources to spend all the money they have on houses, cars, and other forms of property that are considered indicators of status and wealth; but even they have their own challenges to face in life, and comparing your life to theirs will neither help you nor be relevant for the most part to your situation. While it is very easy to desire to have the same lifestyle and acquisitions as the celebrities, it is important to focus on one's own financial situation, stabilizing it, while postponing the accumulation of luxury items until the point one is able to afford them without jeopardizing their finances.

It may one day be possible to have some of those same things if you still want them, but you must first make it through the day and overcome the current situation as it is. Travelling pointlessly and having various unnecessary experiences is not superior to building a strong foundation for a successful life. Other people may be chasing experiences, and they may be putting on a façade, attempting to appear rich and successful, while being secretly and heavily in debt.

However, while you may be, for your own good, resisting the desire to make impulse purchases of luxury items now, you may be able to, once your situation allows it, be able to at least splurge in one category within reason, as long as you do not do so to the extent that you also undo your own progress. For example, you may want fancy cars, yachts, a luxury home, and fancy food; but maybe you will pick only one of those categories to focus on, rather than all at once; and, even for the category you pick, you would live within your means and not lose all your progress, but reward yourself within an acceptable, reasonable, and moderate constraint, as based on your overall financial situation and what would be best for it. Simply staying steady in your goals helps you to make significant strides towards your success.

This applies if you also have friends that live a lavish lifestyle. If your financial situation does not allow it, then there is no reasonable point in trying to keep up, as different people have different capacities to spend money. If it gets to the point where you feel that you are required to explain yourself, then you can simply say that you are working on some financial goals and cannot make such expenditures at this time. No true friend will hold that against you, nor should you try to manipulate them into paying for you. It is also possible that your friend was trying to keep up with you and that you are both in debt.

Anyone who tells you that you are being materialistic for trying to save money and for trying to focus on improving your own financial situation either does not have to worry about their financial security or is taking that security for granted. You would not want to take advice from such a person. Money is more or less the lifeblood of our ability to live in society. One's way of life depends on money and, even when people find themselves living on the fringes of society, whether by choice or not, they find themselves there due to their perception and relationship with money.

In the end, if it comes down to a decision between what other people think of you and your being hopelessly poor due to excessive expenditures, then you are better off not concerning yourself with irrelevant opinions. Work, instead, on making yourself financially strong. Go ahead and turn down invitations to outings you know will be costly. Maybe you could even attempt to substitute the proposed outing plans by suggesting less expensive activities that you would all enjoy.

If you are still concerned about other peoples' opinions in this regard, then consider this: most people respect someone who has their priorities figured out to the point of being financially strong. Most people look up to the rich and successful. If you become rich and successful due to focusing on your priorities and keeping yourself financially strong, then you will also have other peoples' admiration at that point. As for others, they may get jealous, or they may feel inspired to do what you did and make the changes needed in their own life, just as you did for yourself, and, as a result, improve their own lives in the process as well.

www.ingramcontent.com/pod-product-compliance
Lightning Source LLC
Chambersburg PA
CBHW021501210526
45463CB00002B/833